100**CLASSIC**METAL
RIFFSFOR**GUITAR**

Master 100 Rock & Heavy Metal Riffs in The Style of 10 Iconic Rhythm Guitar Players

CHRIS**ZOUPA**

FUNDAMENTAL**CHANGES**

100 Classic Metal Riffs For Guitar

Master 100 Rock & Heavy Metal Riffs in The Style of 10 Iconic Rhythm Guitar Players

ISBN: 978-1-78933-473-9

Published by www.fundamental-changes.com

Copyright © 2025 Chris Zoupa

Edited by Joseph Alexander

For over 350 free guitar lessons with videos check out:

www.fundamental-changes.com

Join our free Facebook Community of Cool Musicians

www.facebook.com/groups/fundamentalguitar

Tag us for a share on Instagram: **FundamentalChanges**

Cover Image: Artwork for Electric Bears for Fundamental Changes Ltd.

Additional drums on audio by Nick Ross

Contents

Introduction

Welcome to *100 Classic Metal Riffs For Guitar*, your one-stop shop for diving into the wild world of legendary rock and metal guitar riffs. In this book, we're going on a riff-fuelled road trip through the styles of the guitar gods, from the father of heavy metal Tony Iommi's doomy swagger, to James Hetfield's machine-gun down-picking, to Alexi Laiho's frantic neo-classical shred, and of course the game-changing flash of Eddie Van Halen.

This is a tongue-in-cheek, riff-by-riff journey that'll beef up your playing and put a mischievous grin on your face (and maybe on your amp, if it had one). If you've ever wondered how these legends create their magic (or just want to learn some badass riffs to annoy your neighbours) you're in the right place, my friend.

What's the game plan? Oh, just 100 riffs in the style of the world's greatest rock and metal guitarists, presented with the kind of irreverent humour and honesty you'd expect from me, your guide, Chris Zoupa.

We'll cover the old-school architects of heavy metal (Black Sabbath and Deep Purple) to thrash titans (Metallica, Megadeth, Slayer) and modern maestros (Children of Bodom, Lamb of God, Killswitch Engage, Periphery). Along the way, you'll pick up the signature techniques that made these players legends. By the time you're done headbanging through these chapters, you'll take your playing from "I can stumble through a Metallica riff if no one's watching", to "I can bust out licks so fiery, other guitarists will wonder if I've been *Running With The Devil*" …and we'll have a hell of a lot of fun doing it.

This book isn't for absolute beginners, it's for intermediate to advanced players who already know their way around a fretboard and are hungry to add some serious sizzle (and maybe a dash of evil) to their playing. Think of it as the secret sauce for transforming solid guitar skills into face-melting prowess. We'll not only learn what these riffs are, but why they work as we dig into how each guitarist approached songwriting and technique. See this as an opportunity to quickly steal their tricks and make them your own (all perfectly legal, I promise).

By the end of this riff odyssey, you'll be able to:

- Chug and bend like a metal god: nail the doom-laden power chords and screaming bends that Tony Iommi pioneered, proving that missing fingertips are no excuse

- Down-pick with attitude: channel your inner Hetfield and gallop on the low strings so hard that your picking hand earns a gym membership. (Warning: down-picking at 200bpm may cause spontaneous combustion… well, maybe some neck spasms and an involuntary "Yeahhh!") Seriously though, take it easy, don't hurt yourself!

- Unleash flashy tricks: harness clever rhythms, the power of muting, and squealing harmonics that make the neighbours think they have a cat infestation.

- Mix melody with madness: blend beautiful melodic runs with chaotic twists *à la* Alexi Laiho and Dave Mustaine. One moment you're sprinkling neo-classical fairy dust, the next you're throwing in a chromatic run or quirky bend that makes everyone double-take

- Groove and djent it up: throw down syncopated riffs and odd-time modern grooves that are chunky enough to make Meshuggah or Misha Mansoor nod in approval – all while keeping things as tight as a duck's butt

And that's just a taste! Each chapter is basically a jam session with a legendary player as your guide. But don't worry, this isn't about turning you into a clone of these guys, it's about understanding how Tony thinks when he writes a riff, how Eddie injects mojo into a chord, or how Hetfield makes even a E5 power chord feel like a punch in the gut. By understanding their mindsets and techniques, you'll not only learn their licks but also how to craft your own in the same spirit.

Throughout the book, expect a lot of humour and brutal honesty. I'll be the cheeky voice on your shoulder saying things like, "Maybe play that one slower, buddy – even Kirk Hammett warms up!" or "If you blow out your amp attempting this Slayer riff, consider it a badge of honour."

We'll keep it light, we'll keep it tight, and we'll keep it fun… because the only thing more metal than nailing a killer riff is doing it with a smile (a slightly evil, Jack-o'-lantern smile, but a smile nonetheless).

So, grab your guitar, turn your amp up to an antisocial volume, and let's get started. Just remember: practice hard, stay loose, and have a blast. These riffs might occasionally make your fingers question their life choices, but hey, if Tony Iommi literally reinvented his playing after losing his fingertips, you can handle a little soreness! Onward to the riff-fest! And don't blame me if you accidentally summon a demon in your living room.

Let's do this!

Chris

I'm writing this in July 2025 and just heard the news.

RIP Ozzy.

Thanks for everything you created.

You touched souls.

Get the Audio

The audio files for this book are available to download for free from **www.fundamental-changes.com.** The link is in the top right-hand corner. Click on the Guitar link then simply select this book title from the drop-down menu and follow the instructions to get the audio.

We recommend that you download the files directly to your computer (not to your tablet or phone) and extract them there before adding them to your media library. If you encounter any difficulty, we provide technical support within 24 hours via the contact form.

For over 350 free guitar lessons with videos check out:

www.fundamental-changes.com

Join our free Facebook Community of Cool Musicians

www.facebook.com/groups/fundamentalguitar

Tag us for a share on Instagram: **FundamentalChanges**

Chapter One – Tony Iommi

"I didn't follow any rules at all. I made my own."

Anthony Frank Iommi Jr. (known to his fans as Tony Iommi) was born on February 19, 1948, in Handsworth, Birmingham, England. He is the co-founder of the heavy metal band Black Sabbath and is hailed as one of the pioneers and creators of the heavy metal genre as a whole.

Tony picked up the guitar in his teens, citing inspiration from Jimi Hendrix as well as Hank Marvin & The Shadows. Only a few years after picking up the instrument, Tony found himself playing in several blues-based rock bands, most notably Earth, which was the early incarnation of Black Sabbath.

Unfortunately for Tony, at age 17 his life and career prospects took a tragic turn. A horrific accident at a sheet metal factory left his right hand disfigured and without fingertips. Tony was sure his guitar-playing days were over, but after discovering the music and story of Django Reinhardt, he was inspired to overcome adversity and give the guitar one more try.

After a brief stint with Jethro Tull, Tony left and reunited with his former Earth bandmates to form Black Sabbath. Black Sabbath's self-titled debut album was released in February 1970, followed by their sophomore release *Paranoid* in September of the same year. *Paranoid* went on to become Black Sabbath's most successful album, selling an astounding 1.6 million copies.

For most of Black Sabbath's debut album, Tony planned to record everything with a Fender Stratocaster. It's worth noting that until this point in his career, Tony had played exclusively on Fender Stratocasters, possibly due to the limited electric guitar options available for left-handed guitarists in 1970s England. During the recording process, however, a faulty neck pickup forced Tony to switch to a different guitar: a Gibson SG. That SG became his signature guitar for the rest of his career.

He used a Laney LA100BL amplifier with a sub-octave undertone, which helped produce the dark, sludgy riffs crucial to Black Sabbath's sound. He was also known to use a Dallas Arbiter Rangemaster to get an extra boost or drive, further dirtying up and saturating his distorted signal.

From legendary riffs and great songs to blistering solos, and one of the meanest tones ever created, Iommi earned praise from the likes of Brian May of Queen, James Hetfield, and Eddie Van Halen, to name a few. My favourite Brian May quote even calls Tony Iommi the "true father of heavy metal", and what an impressive title that is!

Tony Iommi is often hailed as one of the godfathers of heavy metal and a visionary when it comes to dark, sinister riffs. Having created a new musical movement and genre, Tony wrote in his autobiography *Iron Man*, "I didn't follow any rules at all. I made my own."

Recommended Listening

Paranoid – Black Sabbath (1970)

Master of Reality – Black Sabbath (1971)

Heaven and Hell – Black Sabbath (1980)

Dehumanizer – Black Sabbath (1992)

13 – Black Sabbath (2013)

Tony Iommi Riffs

The Tony Iommi-themed ideas I've put together for this chapter are two groups of five riffs, which together make up the sample songs *Tungsten Man* and *War Pork*. The first five are in the key of B Minor with a straight feel, and the second five are in E Minor with a swung feel.

In the first of the five B Minor licks from *Tungsten Man*, you'll combine pedalled, muted chugs on the B root note with inverted 5th double-stops and Tony's signature pentatonic hammer-on fills. The main challenge is the syncopation and picking emphasis, so listen to the audio and follow the upstrokes shown in the notation closely.

Example 1a

In this example, you'll tap into Tony's skill for shifting subdivisions in an instant. From one beat to the next, you move from 1/8th notes to 1/16th notes, then into 1/16th note triplets. The bursts of speed in the middle are best played with hammer-ons and pull-offs on the 5th and 4th strings. This pentatonic phrase needs tight coordination between your index and ring fingers before you fill out the riff with power chords and inverted 5ths. Don't rush the slides, they have a groovy, sludgy feel (you'll know it when you hear it!).

Example 1b

Moving on, here's a riff that highlights Tony's diatonic playing, which is often melodic, slower, and more motif-driven, much like the riffs you hear in Sabbath classics such as *War Pigs* (around 6:34) or *Iron Man* (around 5:01). Lead the first and third bars with your pinky, so the rest of your fingers can handle the melody efficiently. For the second and fourth bars, try leading with either your index or middle finger to see which feels best.

Example 1c

Here's a lick that makes full use of Tony's signature sludgy slide sound and his abrasive unison bends in bar four. The key rhythm to accent is the dotted 1/8th note followed by the 1/16th on the second beat of every bar, as it adds a pickup to what could otherwise be a flat rhythm. You can also hear how riffs like this influenced a young James Hetfield on Metallica's early records. Check out the start of the bridge riff before the outro in Metallica's *Fade to Black* at around 3:53.

Example 1d

In this B Minor riff, you'll play a lick packed with Iommi trademarks, like sliding power chords, minor 7th chords, and a slow, "impending doom" note choice to resolve the phrase. Do not rush the slides, as each has rhythmic value and helps lock in the groove. Isolate the Bm7 barre chord to make sure all the notes ring clearly and are articulated well. Iommi's use of jazzy sounding chords was a clever way to surprise the listener. Blending heavy metal with sophisticated chord ideas was unheard of at the time and still sounds fresh today.

The last bar creates tension by hinting at a G Lydian sound. Heavy metal does not always need the evil b5 to build tension. The #4 (Lydian) interval on the IV chord is worth exploring for creative possibilities.

Example 1e

The next five riffs are swung and in the key of E Minor. Together, they form the sample track *War Pork*.

The first idea combines power chords with hammer-ons. Hold a firm two-string barre to keep clarity between the double-stopped notes and the hammer-ons. You will also need strong, precise legato technique to play the trills in bar eight cleanly.

Example 1f

Next, we'll look at a riff built around a dotted 1/4 note rhythm. This creates interplay between the on and off beats, making the pattern less predictable and adding more swing to the riff. Pay close attention to the placement and strumming of the dead notes, as they come just before an emphatic power chord. Listen to the audio to get a clear feel for the timing.

Example 1g

Here, you'll drift between swung 1/8th notes and triplets, creating a smooth variation in subdivisions. The trickiest part is the picking pattern at the end of each bar. Try ending the triplets on an upstroke so you can land a downstroke at the start of the next bar.

The riff also uses 1/4 tone bends when moving from the 5th to the 4th string, adding movement and attitude. You can hear this technique in the main riff of Pantera's *Revolution Is My Name,* as well as the Eagles classic *Life in the Fast Lane.* It is based mainly around the C# Minor Pentatonic scale to create an Iommi-style shift in key, which is a great way to break the monotony of staying on the E root.

Example 1h

In Example 1i, you'll play a swung, galloping rhythm intertwined with heavy power chords. Melodically this riff is nothing special, but the groove and rhythm are what make it work. Keep the open low E string muted and controlled, so it doesn't ring out and bleed through, and focus on its swung, staccato groove. The picking pattern can feel a bit strange, so pay close attention to the picking directions.

Example 1i

The final example uses a combination of power chord slides and open strings to create variation between the position shifts. This is not a particularly complex riff to play, but the swing element is crucial to making it work. Don't rush the slides as they have rhythmic value and are just as important to the riff as the strummed chords. I strongly suggest switching to your index and ring fingers for the high up the neck power chords to avoid any snug-fingered catastrophes.

Example 1j

Chapter Two – Richie Blackmore

"When you're around someone good, your standards are raised."

Richard Hugh Blackmore was born on April 14, 1945, in Somerset, England and began playing guitar after being given an instrument by his father around the age of 11. He was encouraged to take classical guitar lessons as a condition of receiving the guitar, but quickly grew more interested in the performers of the 1950s and early 1960s. After a rather unhappy period at school, he began further guitar lessons with the highly respected English session guitarist Big Jim Sullivan, and his playing quickly began to draw the attention of other like-minded young musicians.

For most of the early to mid-1960s, Blackmore honed his playing skills in a variety of touring bands, often travelling to Europe and backing well-known artists such as Jerry Lee Lewis. He also undertook a growing amount of session work, most notably for the producer Joe Meek.

With his musical reputation developing rapidly (especially as a fluid improviser and dynamic stage performer), Blackmore was approached to join the fledgling Deep Purple in 1968, alongside organist Jon Lord and drummer Ian Paice. Initially playing a mixture of late '60s pop songs and experimental instrumental music, the early Deep Purple seemed to struggle to find their musical identity, and eventually dismissed their original singer and bassist in an attempt to change their sound.

Blackmore's growing interest in hard rock and lengthy instrumental improvisations eventually became the dominant musical force within the band, and with a new singer and bass guitarist, Purple began recording a series of classic hard rock albums, supported by never-ending tours, that made them international stars and brought them much acclaim for their live shows.

After a second line-up change in 1973, the band continued with more touring and recording until Blackmore, uncomfortable with the changing musical direction of the band, finally left in late 1975 to form Rainbow, the group he stayed with through multiple line-up changes until he re-joined Deep Purple in the mid-1980s. He once again left Deep Purple in 1993, after which he briefly reformed Rainbow before embarking on a lengthy collaboration with his new musical partner (and wife) Candice Night in the Renaissance-influenced acoustic folk group, Blackmore's Night. More recently he has begun to perform hard rock again with a series of concerts playing both Rainbow and Deep Purple songs.

Ritchie Blackmore is commonly associated with playing Fender Stratocasters, although for much of his early career he favoured a Gibson ES-335, before switching to Fenders in the early 1970s. He has used a scalloped neck on his Stratocasters, and this idea has been copied by other hard-rock guitarists such as Yngwie Malmsteen. A keen exponent of using the tremolo arm aggressively on Stratocasters, Blackmore was famous for breaking them in the early Deep Purple days.

Having begun his playing career using smaller, low-wattage combo amplifiers, Blackmore was quick to ally himself with Marshall amplification and was a long-time user of various 100 and 200 watt Marshall heads coupled with 4x12 cabinets. In more recent years he has been using smaller signature combo amplifiers from the Engl company in Germany. Blackmore hasn't been heavily associated with effects units in his playing career, but on occasion he has used a reel-to-reel tape deck as a pre-amp and to provide some delay. Blackmore's sound is full and clear, and not overly distorted in comparison with other hard rock players. He mostly uses the neck and bridge pickups on his Stratocasters, rather than using any pickup combinations.

As with many rock guitarists, Blackmore's dramatic playing style is characterised by a liberal use of Pentatonic and Blues scale patterns, but he also favours less-common scales such as the Harmonic Minor. He makes frequent use of techniques like tremolo picking and wide string bends, coupled with a very distinctive left-hand vibrato. Many of his better-known solos are arpeggio based with a distinct baroque flavour due to his interest in various forms of classical music.

Richie's career, especially early on, was heavily driven by his mentors and keeping company with some of the industry's most elite players. As he said, "When you're around someone good, your standards are raised" – a quote I think we can all get behind. The take-away? Get out of your bedroom and jam with other musicians!

Recommended Listening

In Rock – Deep Purple (1970)

Machine Head – Deep Purple (1972)

Made in Japan – Deep Purple (1972)

Rainbow Rising – Rainbow (1976)

Richie Blackmore Riffs

The Richie Blackmore-themed riffs make up the sample songs *Faces in the Mountains* and *Soul Stealer*. The first five are in E Minor with a straight feel, and the second five are in a swung G Minor.

In the first lick from *Faces in the Mountains*, you'll play a riff based on E Minor Pentatonic in 3rd position. Hammer-ons, slides, vibrato, and palm mutes are used throughout to add interest and dynamics. Try to play most of the riff with your index and ring fingers.

Example 2a

The next example explores Richie's use of octaves and arpeggiated chord movements. Play the 1/8th note at the end of each bar with an upstroke to keep the rhythm and groove consistent.

Example 2b

This riff uses three-string triad voicings that fit perfectly in the 1970s classic rock sound and helped pave the way for the glam and heavy metal movements of the 1980s. You can hear this approach in the rhythm parts of players like Eddie Van Halen, Yngwie Malmsteen, and Randy Rhoads.

Be mindful of the dead notes and use them to keep the momentum in your strumming arm. You will also want to use a flat ring finger on any chords that have three notes on the same fret.

Example 2c

This idea is based around a combination of single notes and inverted 5th power chords which Richie loved writing. In fact, this concept began a style of riff writing that inspired Van Halen and early '80s Metallica.

What keeps this riff interesting is the use of grace notes slides that tie together the first two bars as well as bars five and six. The entry of these slides is on the final off beat 1/8th note, so you'll need keep them tight to highlight the brief moment of syncopation.

Example 2d

The final riff of this group uses a combination of hammer-ons, double stops, four-string chord triads, as well as a cool single-note fill.

Although it appears riddled with different concepts, they're all relatively easy to play. The trickiest part is the use of dead notes to help with position shifts, while emphasising the syncopation on the double-stops and sus4 chords. Bottom line: Pay attention to the strumming directions.

Example 2e

The next five riffs are in the key of G Minor and have a deeply swung feel. Together, they form the sample track *Soul Stealer*.

The first idea capitalises on Richie's love of inverted 5th chords and is an homage to many of his excellent riffs. Play the 3rd fret on the 6th string with your thumb, Hendrix-style, to leave the other fingers free for the double-stops. The quick subdivision shifts between the swung 1/8th notes to the triplet 1/8th notes can be a little tricky. Check out the audio to get the feel and groove.

Example 2f

This riff is a tribute to Richie's love of pedalled bluesy licks which, dare I say it, contain a bit of Country fusion.

The fretted G will need to be held and pedalled between the melody. Use an index finger barre on the 3rd fret if you wish, but this runs the risk of unwanted notes bleeding into one another. I personally recommend you try the Hendrix thumb approach used above.

Example 2g

This line capitalises Blackmore's signature, swung groove. To keep the moderate gallop consistent, use entirely alternate picking as it's much harder to create a swung bounce with just down strokes. Have a listen to the audio and pay close attention to the flow of the riff.

Example 2h

Now we'll use E Minor Pentatonic to create a groovy, heavy-blues riff. The most important parts of this riff are the inverted 5th double-stops and the swing between the 5th and 7th frets.

You'll notice that the picking direction on the notation dictates *outside* picking, as you need to use an upstroke on the 5th fret on the D string, followed by a downstroke on the A string, to not get trapped by the strings.

Example 2i

The final riff focuses on muted notes and an interplay between 3rds and suspended 4ths within a triad riff. There are different fingerings for the triad chords based on the 6th string then the 5th. Play the root note of the G and Gsus4 chords with a Hendrixian thumb wrapped around the neck.

Example 2j

Chapter Three – Eddie Van Halen

"If you want to be a rock star or just be famous, run down the street naked; you'll make the news or something. But if you want music to be your livelihood, then play, play, play and play! Eventually you'll get where you want to be."

Edward Lodewijk Van Halen (more commonly known as Eddie Van Halen) was born on January 26, 1955, in Amsterdam, the Netherlands. Edward's father was Dutch, a jazz multi-instrumentalist who encouraged him and his brother Alex (co-founder and drummer of Van Halen) to play classical piano from a very young age. Around the age of 11, Edward first picked up the guitar. He cites Eric Clapton as his earliest source of inspiration and influence. Eddie was also a fan of the guitar playing of Jimmy Page, Ritchie Blackmore, and Allan Holdsworth. (You can clearly see the Holdsworth influence in some of Eddie's alien-like hand stretches!)

Edward founded his first band, Mammoth, in 1972 with his brother Alex. They were eventually joined by singer David Lee Roth in 1974 and changed the band's name to Van Halen. Van Halen went on to release their debut album in 1978, simply titled *Van Halen* (often referred to as Van Halen I). That record is still widely regarded as one of the best hard-rock debut albums of all time. It immediately established Van Halen as one of the greatest rock bands on the planet. (Let's not forget this album contained the epic track *Eruption,* with arguably the greatest guitar solo ever recorded!)

The band saw incredible mainstream success with the release of their sixth studio album, *1984,* an album that perfectly showcased the band's polished songwriting, catchy melodies, and Edward's incredible guitar playing. It contained the hits *Hot for Teacher, Jump,* and *Panama,* which remain timeless classics, still enjoyed by fans and music lovers over four decades later.

There was a distinct character to Eddie's tone that became known in rock lore as *the Brown Sound.* Simply put, it was a harsh, heavily overdriven signal (sometimes paired with a phaser) that still somehow had a liquidity and warmth. He would achieve this tone by playing through Marshall amplifiers or his own signature Peavey 5150 amp, and by using his modded Kramer guitar with the stock single-coil removed and a humbucker pickup installed, creating his iconic Frankenstrat.

Eddie changed the world of electric guitar in the same way visionaries like Django Reinhardt and Jimi Hendrix did. He influenced and helped pave the way for guitarists like Nuno Bettencourt, Joe Satriani, John Mayer, Zakk Wylde, Mike McCready (Pearl Jam), Slash, and countless others. John Mayer once said that Eddie Van Halen was a guitar superhero; a true virtuoso; a stunningly good musician and composer. It's very difficult to argue with that statement.

That being so, Eddie's greatest qualities were his work ethic and, most importantly, his humility. He was willing to work hard and was more interested in creating and playing music than being famous for its own sake.

Recommended Listening

Van Halen – Van Halen (1978, often referred to as Van Halen I)

Fair Warning – Van Halen (1981)

1984 – Van Halen (1984)

5150 – Van Halen (1986)

For Unlawful Carnal Knowledge – Van Halen (1991)

Eddie Van Halen Riffs

The Eddie Van Halen-themed riffs in this chapter are presented as two groups of five that make up the sample songs *Ice Cream Cake* and *Detethered*. The first five examples are in Eb Standard tuning (Eb Ab Db Gb Bb Eb) with a swung feel, and the second five are in Drop C# (C# G# C# F# A# D#) with a straight feel.

In the first of these Eb Standard riffs, you will combine relatively open chord shapes with arpeggiations and picking sequences, creating interplay between major triads and sus4 chords for movement and tension – a hallmark Eddie technique.

Where possible, play the open A and D shapes with barred fingers to free up others for hammer-ons and pull-offs on the sus4 notes. The riff resolves in bar eight with natural harmonics, which stand out best when using the bridge pickup and picking close to the bridge, where the tighter string tension produces a clearer, more resonant ping.

Example 3a

For the next lick, you will play a chordal variation on the progression in Example 3a, similar to the kind of riff Van Halen might use when the full band kicks in for the first time. Focus on the contrast between big open chords and tightly palm muted chords, as the mix of ringing sustain and percussive chugs creates much of the riff's drive and excitement. To finish, the lick moves into a rolling legato harmonic effect. Play a three-note legato figure on the D string with your fretting hand, then let the side of your picking hand palm glide lightly along the string. If done smoothly, you will hear a sequence of shifting harmonics as you move toward the bridge.

Example 3b

This riff blends open pedal notes with a classic EVH groove, paired with dyads on the 5th and 4th strings in intervals of 3rds and 4ths. These two note shapes, heard in tracks like *Hot for Teacher* and *Runnin' with the Devil*, add colour and variation beyond standard power chords – essential for keeping riffs engaging. Once you have this example under your fingers, try writing your own Van Halen inspired riff by combining a pedalled open note with alternate dyad shapes. Pay close attention to the picking directions marked in the notation, as they have a big impact on the bounce and swing of the groove. You can also experiment with hybrid picking on the dyads to add a sharper, chicken pickin' snap.

Example 3c

Here you will work through a riff built on inverted 5th double-stops, similar to the chorus of *Somebody Get Me a Doctor*. Fret each double-stop with flat fingers and aim for even clarity between both notes of the chord. If any notes sound muted or weak, use a firmer, flatter grip on the fretboard. Pay close attention to the hammer-ons in bars three and seven, playing them with extra force to keep the riff's energy and bite intact.

Example 3d

In this final *Ice Cream Cake* lick, the groove is driven by an anacrusis that falls on the "2&" of the bar. Keep your fretting hand anchored in the 1st position of the A Minor Pentatonic scale, stepping outside the shape only for the chord stabs in bars five, eight, and nine. For the quick sus4 to triad move in bar five, use a flattened index finger to make the transition smooth and efficient.

Example 3e

These five riffs are in Drop C# tuning with a straight rhythmic feel, and together they form my sample track *Detethered*.

The first combines low, drop-tuned chug chords with Eddie's preference for brighter midrange voicings on the 2nd, 3rd, and 4th strings. The progression moves between triads and suspended shapes to create tension and flow, as shown in the notation. Barre the 7th fret chords with a flat index finger, and use your pinky for the sus4 shapes unless you find it more practical to barre with your ring finger when moving into the A triad. Following the suggested fingering will help keep transitions smooth and controlled.

Example 3f

Now let's channel Eddie's funky yet heavy verse riff style, as heard in *5150* and *Unchained*. The main groove combines 1/4 tone bluesy bends for grit and attitude with inverted 5th power chords that add weight without muddying the harmony. At the tail of the riff, natural harmonics provide a sharp tonal accent.

Keep the fingers playing the double-stop as flat as possible, so both notes sustain evenly, adjusting pressure if one starts to fade. In bar eight, strike the harmonics right on the edge of the fret wire rather than the centre to produce a bright, cutting chime. Picking closer to the bridge will make them even clearer.

Example 3g

This line uses three note chord shapes in Eddie's trademark mid to upper-mid register, similar to the ideas explored in Ritchie Blackmore's chapter. Let the arpeggiated notes ring into one another to create a loose, rolling texture. As in the pre chorus of *Panama*, avoid being overly precise or using heavy palm muting with the picking hand, allowing the chords to breathe and overlap naturally.

Example 3h

A cool EVH trick is to move between four string triads and inverted 5th double-stops. While the overall structure here is straightforward, the arpeggiated run in bar four and the raked chords in bars 8-9 demand precise, deliberate arching of the fretting hand. Done correctly, this will let each note ring clearly and sustain while preventing unwanted noise, muted notes, or squeaks.

Example 3i

Finally, this riff blends arpeggiated and strummed chords for a classic Van Halen texture. In Drop C# tuning, Eddie could create more interplay between the 5th, suspended 2nd, and major or minor 3rd intervals within power chord shapes. Many of the chord voicings here use adjacent or repeated fret positions, so follow the suggested fingering to keep transitions smooth and allow quick shifts between chord variations.

Example 3j

Chapter Four – James Hetfield

"I was pretty much afraid of everything. Afraid of the world. Afraid of speaking (just a really, really shy kid). Music was a way to speak, as simple as that. That's me telling the world about me when I can't do it on my own... Music was the voice I didn't have."

James Alan Hetfield was born on August 3, 1963, in Downey, California, USA. Over the past four decades, Hetfield has been the main songwriter and rhythm guitarist in the band Metallica.

James first picked up the guitar at the age of 14, having previously dabbled in drums and piano. It wasn't long before he joined a few bands in high school, namely Leather Charm and Obsession. All of these high school band endeavours eventually dissolved (let's face it, they usually do). In 1981, Hetfield founded Metallica with Lars Ulrich.

After the tumultuous firing of Dave Mustaine and the quick poaching of then-Exodus lead guitarist Kirk Hammett, Metallica recorded and released their debut album *Kill 'Em All* in 1983. The album featured obvious nods to the New Wave of British Heavy Metal movement as well as classic Punk. The release of *Kill 'Em All* was pivotal and a blueprint for the Thrash Metal sound that would dominate the metal scene throughout the '80s.

In 1991, Metallica pivoted away from their iconic thrash sound, which had been driven by technicality and speed. James and the band focused more on genuine songwriting and vulnerability, creating stadium rock bangers. This shift resulted in the release of the *Black Album*, which sold over 30 million copies and solidified Metallica as one of the greatest heavy metal bands of all time.

Throughout his career, James Hetfield has usually opted to play Gibson or ESP Explorer guitars. His signature Explorer built by Ken Lawrence Custom Guitars is his current weapon of choice. He also uses Mesa Boogie and Marshall heads to get his unique and untouchably tight, aggressive rhythm sound.

His contribution to rock and the metal world is undeniable, inspiring generations of guitarists and bands, and making Metallica one of the biggest and most influential music groups of all time.

Recommended Listening

Ride The Lightning – Metallica (1984)

Master of Puppets – Metallica (1986)

...And Justice for All – Metallica (1988)

Self-Titled (Black Album) – Metallica (1991)

Death Magnetic – Metallica (2008)

James Hetfield Riffs

The James Hetfield-themed riffs I've put together for this chapter are organised into two groups of five riffs that make up the sample songs *Last Keeper of the Light* and *Don't Kill Everyone*.

The first example is an arpeggiated riff inspired by some classic Metallica ballads. Be mindful of the ringing open strings in each arpeggiation, as often these triads can build dissonance. When handled with care, however, they can add emotion and a melodic complexity.

Use your pinky finger as much as possible as it's the easiest one to arch while letting the open notes ring.

Example 4a

Next, we'll look at a riff based on James' love for driving mid-riff gallops. Most of this riff uses downstroke 1/8th notes to keep it as heavy and Hetfield-like as possible. The riff gets interesting when 1/16th notes occur, as they create the gallop that should be played with alternate picking.

Example 4b

In Example 4c you'll navigate jumps between regular and inverted power chords, all riddled with string changes. Play this riff with a click track, focusing on creating tight, aggressive changes between 1/4 and 1/8th note subdivisions.

This kind of chord-driven idea is probably more suited to a chorus section with vocals that follow the rhythm of the chordal movements.

Example 4c

This lick contains a key-change idea and suddenly modulates up a whole step from E to F# which creates melodic interest, especially as the tonic (open) string has begun every riff and section of the song thus far.

The most challenging part is the transition and position shift between bars seven and eight. Use the pull-off from the 2nd fret to give your hand time for the position shift. Lead the slide at the 7th fret with your index finger and you should be able to play the entire fill (or turnaround) without your pinky.

Example 4d

For the final riff in this group of five, you'll be exploring Hetfield's love of b5 (flat five) intervals to create bluesy-sounding, heavy riffs. What makes this riff interesting is the use of dead notes to emphasise the syncopation, as well as slides into the 6th fret that give the b5 interval a more dynamic entry. Although we slide into the 6th fret in almost every bar, the fingering differs depending on what follows, so pay attention to my suggested fingering.

Example 4e

The next five riffs come together to create the sample track *Don't Kill Everyone*. They're played predominantly in the key of A Minor, occasionally modulating to E.

This next riff is inspired by Hetfield's early '80s love of inverted 5th chords (possibly in turn inspired by Blackmore). You'll combine these chords with open chugs and pentatonic notes, as well as an added b5 interval. Play all inverted 5th chords with a flat finger, aiming for clear note articulation and clean hammer-ons.

Example 4f

Let's expand the previous idea, but now with E as our riff centre to create a tonal shift. The motifs and ideas are similar but sound darker in the lower key.

Example 4g

This chorus idea is based on power chords with easy motifs that would give space for the singer. Pay close attention to the use of 1/4 note power chords in bars four and eight, as well as a stylish use of chromaticism. Sync with the drums and try not to rush!

Example 4h

Next, you'll play a riff using James' gallops and his fast-moving inverted 5th chords. If gallops are tricky, loop a click track and play the open E string with the rhythms from bars one, three, five, and seven. I count them as one "straw-ber-ry" per beat. Nailing this rhythm helped me play *Battery* and many Iron Maiden songs, so it's worth drilling. Follow the suggested picking pattern in the notation.

Example 4i

This final riff mixes gallops and pull-offs. Keep the timing and swing in mind. I think of it as a fast-paced pirate shanty! In bars seven and eight, there's a sudden key change from A to E, which throws the listener a curveball. It may sound daunting, but try writing your own riff with a sudden key shift. You could use the same formula: six bars in one key, then move up a 5th or down a 4th for the last two bars.

Example 4j

Chapter Five – Dave Mustaine

"What I couldn't say verbally I was able to express physically with the guitar."

David Scott Mustaine (known colloquially as Dave or Megadave) was born on September 13, 1961, in La Mesa, California, USA. He is known throughout the metal community as the Godfather of Thrash Metal, being one of the main contributors to the Big 4 of Thrash movement in the 1980s. He is best known as the founder, guitarist, and songwriter of the thrash metal band Megadeth, and he was also Metallica's first lead guitarist (before Kirk Hammett).

Mustaine's guitar journey began at the age of 13, when he took lessons from his older sister's boyfriends. He was primarily self-taught, citing influences like Budgie, Iron Maiden, Motorhead, and anything from the New Wave of British Heavy Metal genre. He also says he grew up listening to lots of Motown records and attributes Megadeth's swing and bounce in his riff writing to those early influences.

Dave's first band, Panic, was where he began honing what would become Megadeth's sound (as well as influencing early Metallica) with fast, groovy, heavy riffs. This band came to a tragic end when multiple members were killed in separate alcohol and drug related motor vehicle accidents.

After his brief stint in Metallica, Mustaine was fired in 1983 and set out to form his own revenge band, initially titled (rather unfortunately) Fallen Angels, which thankfully quickly changed its name to Megadeth.

Megadeth released their debut album *Killing Is My Business... and Business Is Good!* in 1985. Although the album's production wasn't anything to get particularly excited about, the raw aggression, speed and musicianship certainly got the band (and a very vengeful Dave Mustaine) plenty of attention. This release, along with their intense live shows, immediately cemented Megadeth as a driving force, helping to propel the evolution of the New Wave of British Heavy Metal into the American thrash scene.

By 1992, Megadeth had released four studio albums, each receiving praise for its technicality as well as Mustaine's inventive arrangements and songwriting prowess. Their fifth studio album *Countdown to Extinction* was a huge commercial success, selling 2.4 million copies. This album incorporated more rock elements and emotion, with Mustaine tackling some very vulnerable topics, from dealing with his inner demons to calling out corruption in politics.

Throughout the years, Mustaine has played guitars from Jackson and Dean, mostly favouring V-shaped bodies. In 2021, he struck up a partnership with Gibson and even released his own signature model, the Silver Metallic V.

Dave's lengthy career, spanning more than four decades, has always shown a devotion to Marshall amps, especially their cabs and the JCM800 and JVM410H heads. He also had a short-lived partnership with Line 6 in the late 2000s, but that brief deviation was hardly pivotal to his signature sound.

Mustaine's legacy is extensive as he played in two of the bands in the Big 4 of Thrash Metal, and he even briefly worked with Slayer's Kerry King during King's short tenure in Megadeth. Many musicians in the scene, as well as diehard fans, have dubbed Dave Mustaine the Godfather of Thrash.

Former bandmate Marty Friedman has high praise for Dave's rhythm playing and riff writing. He even noted the specifics of Mustaine's palm muting, calling it very unique and very important to the sound of Megadeth.

Mustaine often comes across as a socially awkward yet introspective genius, but as an artist who's spent much of his career being misunderstood, he has still managed to redefine the face of Metal guitar.

Recommended Listening

Peace Sells... but Who's Buying? – Megadeth (1986)

Rust in Peace – Megadeth (1990)

Countdown to Extinction – Megadeth (1992)

United Abominations – Megadeth (2007)

Dystopia – Megadeth (2016)

Dave Mustaine Riffs

The Dave Mustaine-themed riffs I've put together for this chapter form the sample songs *Kingdom of Dirt* and *Dystopian Warhead*. The first five riffs are played in A Dorian/A Phrygian with a straight feel, and the second five are played with a swung feel in F# Minor.

In the first of five riffs from *Kingdom of Dirt*, you'll use hammer-ons and alternate-picked 1/16th notes. Keep your wrist loose but controlled for the alternate picking, and dig in a bit harder on the hammer-ons and pull-offs so they stand out dynamically.

Example 5a

In this lick, you'll play a riff built on chugged open notes and basic power chords. The bounce comes from the dotted and tied notes in bars one, three, five, and seven. When learning tricky rhythms, I find the best approach is to get familiar with them first.

A useful exercise is to play the whole riff with only dead notes, as removing the melody forces you to lock in the rhythm and notice the note values more clearly.

Example 5b

Example 5c is based on Dave's use of dotted 1/8th rhythms and pentatonic b5 fills. I usually play power chords with my pinky, but in this case I recommend using your index and ring fingers because of how the fills sit in the riff. The timing here is full of variety and includes floating dotted 1/8ths, fast 1/16ths, and triplet 1/4 notes. Listen to the audio a few times to lock in the phrasing and timing.

Example 5c

This lick is built on Dave's blend of New Wave of British Heavy Metal and Motown swing. It's not hard to play and doesn't rely on heavy theory, but the timing and emphasis can be tricky. Bars two and six start with a dotted 1/8th note into a 1/16th which is a classic Mustaine structure, and one that set him apart from other '80s thrash players. Bars four and eight finish with arpeggios in slow 1/4-note triplets, which are easier if you stick to the suggested fingering.

Example 5d

Here's a signature Mustaine arpeggiated clean section that works well as an introduction or bridge. The arpeggios are mainly five-string patterns that follow a fairly predictable string sequence. Keep your fretting hand arched so the open strings ring out, keeping the mood mysterious and melancholy. For listening homework, check out *In My Darkest Hour*, *Trust*, and the introduction to Metallica's *The Call of Ktulu*, which Dave wrote while in the band.

Example 5e

The next five riffs are in F# Minor with a swung feel and form the sample track *Dystopian Warhead*. The first uses chromatically descending power chords with a 1/4 note triplet emphasis, with accents on bars one, two, five, and six.

The rest combines single-note hammer-ons with an 1/8th note triplet feel. The hardest part is the transition at the end of bar four. Use a slide into the 9th fret power chord to make it seamless.

Example 5f

Here's a lick that makes the most of the swing feel and the crazy dynamic shifts created by quick changes in subdivisions. Granted, there are some fiddly parts, but the hardest thing is to lock in with the swing. Pay close attention to the strumming directions for bars one, three, five, and seven in the notation.

Example 5g

Now move on to Example 5h. This riff is based on pedalling root notes mixed with major and minor 3rd dyads and tritones. The hardest part is keeping the triplet swing steady while jumping from the 6th string to the dyads on the 3rd and 4th strings without sounding rushed or clunky. The suggested strumming and fingering in the notation should help make this outrageous and "Mustainious" (a word I just coined!) riff easier to play.

Example 5h

Now we'll look at a lick using 1/4 note triplets to outline a chord movement. There's also a clear shift in feel, as this idea is based around A Dorian. If you can, let the notes briefly bleed into each other for a more arpeggiated sound. Listen to the audio to hear the phrasing. I've loosely added the inferred chord names above each bar to show what I had in mind when writing this riff.

Example 5i

Lastly, here's a lick that demonstrates ways to create riffs using the minor pentatonic scale, in this case F# Minor, while splicing in the 2nd and b5 intervals. Since most of the riff sits between the 2nd and 5th frets, use one finger per fret. I've given a suggested fingering in the notation.

Example 5j

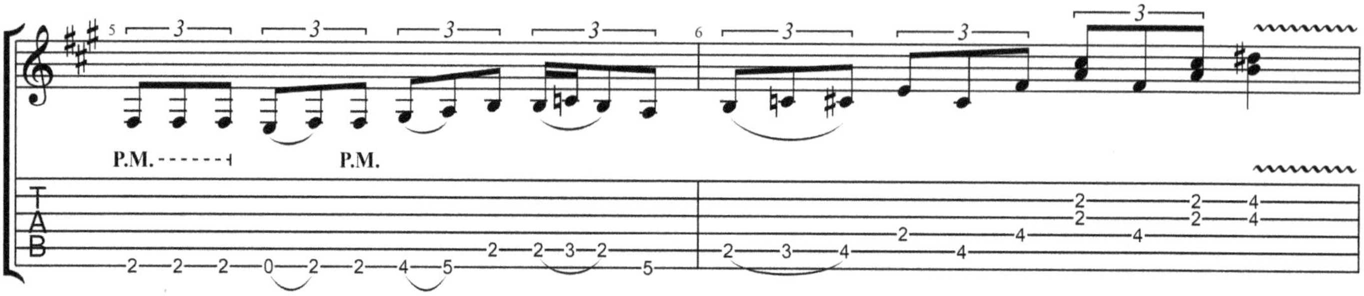
P.M.
P.M.

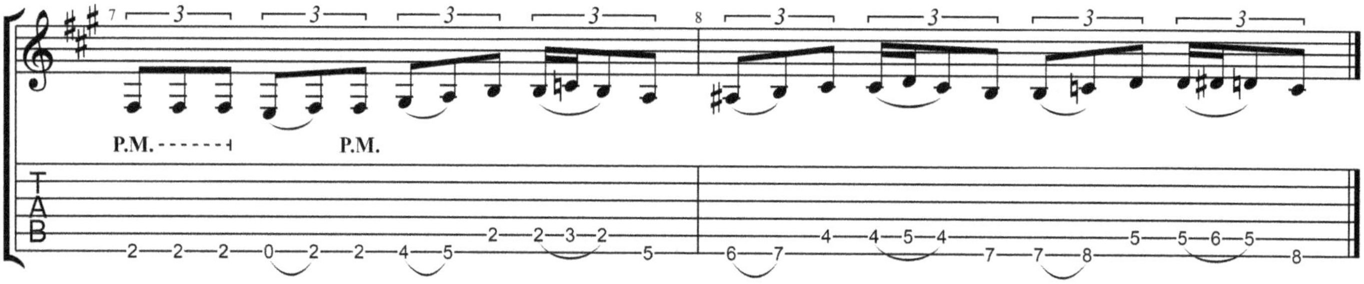
P.M.
P.M.

Chapter Six – Jeff Hanneman

"I like playing guitar, I don't like talking about it. I like writing riffs, I don't like explaining them."

Jeffrey John Hanneman was born on January 31, 1964, in Long Beach, California, USA. He was one half of the guitar duo in the thrash metal band Slayer, and his riffs and songwriting craftsmanship can be heard on some of the band's most famous songs

Jeff began playing guitar at the age of twelve, citing hardcore punk bands like Black Flag, Wasted Youth, and Dead Kennedys as some of his biggest influences. Jeff honed his craft without any formal lessons and often stated he was entirely self-taught. This likely helped forge his evil, dissonant and often rule-breaking riffing and songwriting style.

Jeff co-founded his first and only band, Slayer, in 1981 with fellow axeman Kerry King. Slayer signed with Metal Blade Records and released their debut album *Show No Mercy* in 1983. The album was met with some seriously negative reviews, but somehow it became Metal Blade's highest-selling release of that year. Slayer later released *South of Heaven* in 1988. It was the band's first album to include a slow song, as well as some moments of experimentation that wavered from typical thrash tropes. That album sold about 610,000 copies and remains Slayer's highest-selling album to date.

Jeff's aggressive tone and playing style were a trademark of Slayer's overall sound. He used predominantly ESP guitars, including his custom Heineken signature LTD JH-600EC (a Les Paul-shaped model), as well as his camo-finish ESP JH-UC (a super-strat shape). These guitars, combined with cranked Marshall amps and EMG 81 active pickups, would be enough to make even the wimpiest guitarist sound monstrous!

Jeff was taken from us early, and was mourned deeply by the thrash metal community he had been so influential in shaping.

"He wrote some of the greatest riffs of all time" – Alex Skolnick (Testament)

"Unassuming, but when the music started he would go 0 to 1000! He would go out there and just destroy every night" – Corey Taylor (Slipknot, Stone Sour)

Jeff himself was a quiet man of few words, not hell-bent on the spotlight or glory. He just loved music, loved his instrument, and loved being able to share it with whoever was willing to listen. The opening quote in this chapter perfectly sums him up.

Recommended Listening

Reign in Blood – Slayer (1986)

South of Heaven – Slayer (1988)

Seasons in the Abyss – Slayer (1990)

God Hates Us All – Slayer (2001)

Christ Illusion – Slayer (2006)

Jeff Hanneman Riffs

The Jeff Hanneman-themed riffs in this chapter form the sample songs *North of Heck* and *Insert Morbid Pun Here*. Both are in Eb Standard tuning (Eb Ab Db Gb Bb Eb) with tempos of 186bpm and 175bpm. The first five riffs are built around a droning open low E string, while the second set are rooted on F# to show how Slayer often uses a fretted root note.

In the first of the five E-drone riffs from *North of Heck*, you'll use palm-muted 1/16th notes on the open low string to build pace and tension, then 1/8th note power chord stabs for variety. Keep as little tension as possible in your wrist and forearm during the fast open note runs, as it's easy to slip into bad technique.

For practice, play along with the sample audio and focus on the click track and drums as much as you can.

Example 6a

The second idea uses a driving 1/8th note pulse and combines power chords with major and minor dyads. Watch out for the chromatic descending dyads in bar four, and keep your fretting hand extra arched on the 1st fret power chord, so that the open 5th string rings clearly. Bars 7-8 switch to single-note riffage. Get your pinky involved on the legato phrase when playing the 5th fret note.

Example 6b

This riff uses Slayer-style note choices, mixing the F# Phrygian scale with an emphasis on the b2, and the F# Harmonic Minor scale with an emphasis on the major 7th. It's a flurry of pedalled 1/16th notes spliced with a few string skips. Stay in one hand position if you can, with each finger covering the 2nd to 5th frets. Play the 1/16th notes with strict alternate picking and the 1/8th notes with strict down picking.

Example 6c

Now we have a riff based on Slayer's use of chromaticism and evil-sounding power chords. Watch the placement of the galloped rhythms in the odd-numbered bars. I call these the "apple pie" gallop, as they use two 1/16th notes followed by one 1/8th note which you can articulate by saying, guess what, "apple pie"! Keep your wrist loose so you can fire off these gallops whenever needed. We'll use this rhythm grouping again in a later chapter on Willie Adler's playing style.

Example 6d

In the final riff of this first group, you'll combine quick hammer-ons, open string notes and inverted 5th power chords. Inspired by the bridge in Slayer's *Angel of Death*, it's packed with both technique and melody but works best in half time, locking in with the drum groove. The trills in bar six are the trickiest part and should be played with your index and middle fingers. Listen closely to the drums and hear how everything fits together in the full track.

Example 6e

The next five riffs make up my track *Insert Morbid Pun Here*. This first riff is almost entirely steady 1/8th notes, with just one 1/4 note at the end of bar four. Play as many of the picked notes as you can with downstrokes. You'll hear a nasty tritone power chord in bars two and four that pulls off to the 2nd fret. Whether you usually fret power chords with your index and pinky, or index and ring, is up to you, but lead this tritone with your middle finger.

Example 6f

For the next lick, we'll play a simple, almost bassline-like melody on the two lowest strings. What makes this riff fun (and challenging) is its tremolo-like burst of 1/16th notes. For tremolo picking, keep your wrist loose, your forearm stable but relaxed, and make the pendulum motion of your picking as small as possible to boost speed and accuracy.

Example 6g

51

In this riff you'll alternate between single notes and chords, drifting in and out of palm muting. It leans heavily on the b5 interval (the "devil's interval" tritone) and uses both power chords and 4th dyad chords (inverted 5ths). Most of it is made up of relentless 1/8th notes. To keep it aggressive and thrash-sounding, aim for as much down picking as possible. Your arm will get tired if you play riffs like this for too long, so take breaks and never push through the pain. Your picking endurance and down picking strength will build up over time.

Example 6h

The following riff is a haunting, *South of Heaven*-inspired lick that focuses more on melody than speed. It features a repetitious melody and an implied chord movement on the 6th and 5th strings. To keep it as evil-sounding as possible, play the whole thing with downstrokes and make a clear contrast between the palm-muted chugs and the big open chords in bar eight.

Example 6i

52

Finally, let's tackle a riff that draws on Jeff Hanneman's use of lightning-fast 1/16th note runs paired with inverted power chords. This is the kind of riff you might hear as the backing rhythm under a wild Slayer solo, and it's one of the few times I'd suggest not palm muting the single note runs to keep the whole riff open and aggressive. Keep your wrist loose and avoid tensing your elbow or forearm. If you feel tension building, take a break and try some finger and wrist stretches before carrying on.

Example 6j

Chapter Seven – Alexi Laiho

"I need chaos around me to feel comfortable."

Alexi Laiho was born on April 8, 1979, in Espoo, Finland. He is known for his guitar work in the bands Children of Bodom and Sinergy, and was a pioneer as a composer and instrumentalist in the power/melodic metal and neo-classical world.

Alexi began his musical journey at age 7 on the violin. He switched to electric guitar at age 11, when he got his first guitar (and no, it wasn't a power metal axe of destiny, it was simply a Tokai Stratocaster copy).

His amazing playing style can be attributed to his love of classic metal bands like Judas Priest, Manowar, and Helloween, as well as his admiration for virtuosic guitarists like Steve Vai and Yngwie Malmsteen.

Alexi formed a band called IneartheD in 1993, which later changed its name to Children of Bodom. They released their debut album *Something Wild* in 1997. It was clear from the start that Alexi's playing was out of this world, and his approach to power metal was something the metal community was keen to keep an eye on.

In 2000, Children of Bodom released their third album, *Follow the Reaper*. The album was met with high praise and significantly higher sales compared to their previous releases. This led the band to earn a gold certification in their native Finland. *Follow the Reaper* set the band on a trajectory of success and cemented Laiho as one of the most influential guitar players of that era.

Alexi was a longtime ESP player and had his own signature Arrow V model, heavily influenced by the original Randy Rhoads V shape and design. He would drift between Marshall and ENGL amp heads, but more often than not opted for a Marshall 4x12 cab.

Alexi made waves very early on in his career, catching the attention of Kirk Hammett, Matt Heafy, Mark Morton (Lamb of God), Herman Li (DragonForce), and many others.

Dave Mustaine described him as, "A gentle spirit with an amazing talent." Upon Alexi's passing, Mustaine remarked, "Now heaven's heavy metal band has a lead guitarist."

Alexi's lifestyle and compositions portrayed him as a very restless artist, seemingly incapable of inner peace. His desire to chase chaos and live life on the edge ultimately caught up with him and he passed away at just 41 years old.

Recommended Listening

Hatebreeder – Children of Bodom (1999)

Follow the Reaper – Children of Bodom (2000)

To Hell and Back – Sinergy (2000)

Hate Crew Death Roll – Children of Bodom (2003)

Halo of Blood – Children of Bodom (2013)

Alexi Laiho Riffs

The Alexi Laiho-themed riffs in this chapter are again split into two groups of five, making up the example tracks *I Am the Warchild* and *Car Crash, Blood Fight*. The first five are in D Standard tuning (D G C F A D) with a fast, thrashier feel, while the second five are in Drop C (C G C F A D) with more focus on groove and chunk.

In the first of five D Standard licks from *I Am the Warchild*, you'll use power chords, major and minor 3rd dyads, and open notes to keep the pace between chords. Pay attention to the galloped rhythm (1/16th + 1/16th + 1/8th) in the odd-numbered bars. At 101bpm, it's worth warming up with a metronome by playing open muted notes in the galloped rhythm. Get comfortable with this before adding the chords and learning the full riff.

Example 7a

This idea is based on Alexi's love of mid-riff chromaticism. For the most part it uses straightforward power chords with a galloped rhythm, so your focus should be on bars two and six. Use all four fingers on the chromatic descents to keep it as smooth, articulate, and muted as possible.

Example 7b

The following riff uses major and minor 3rd dyads as a more melodic alternative to power chords. You'll also play single note riffage that makes use of open notes and hammer-ons for speed and flair. The trickiest part is the pull-offs in bars two and four. Keep your index finger firmly on the 7th fret of the 5th string, and alternate between your pinky and ring fingers for the legato notes.

Example 7c

Next we'll look at a melodic riff based on pedalling root notes and moving between the root and the inverted 5th of each implied chord. Flatten your index finger to fret the adjacent strings and use your other fingers for the melodic parts. Watch out for the string skips in bars three and seven.

Example 7d

Now move on to Example 7e. This riff uses two very cool, quintessential Alexi moves: a tempo change and a sudden switch from a straight feel to a swung feel. Once swung, it is full of 1/8th note triplets. You will also hear open notes on the 1st and 2nd strings mixed with arpeggios and two-string diatonic runs. Pay close attention to the picking directions in the first bar. Apart from the legato notes, everything is down picked to keep the triplet emphasis solid and predictable.

Example 7e

The next five riffs are in Drop C tuning and form the sample track *Car Crash, Blood Fight*. In the first of these ideas, you'll play a riff based on an Iron Maiden-style gallop made up of one 1/8th note followed by two 1/16th notes. You'll shift from muted single notes to ringing minor triads and octave chords, creating a clear contrast between the dynamics. Since you're playing with distortion, keep any unplayed strings muted and controlled.

Example 7f

Next, you'll play a fast-paced but straightforward metal riff that blends palm-muted sections, gallops, hammer-ons, and chords. Bar two ends with a short lick that moves from a minor triad into a diminished triad. Play this with strict alternate picking and use all four fingers of your fretting hand, spanning the 5th to the 8th frets.

Example 7g

The following riff is a mid-range melodic line inspired by the neo-classical side of Alexi's playing. Bars two and four finish with mid-riff arpeggio shapes that are easy to play if you follow the notated fingering. Keep your picking alternate to emphasise melody over aggression and create a controlled rather than chaotic sound.

Example 7h

Next, move on to Example 7i. This riff is a single-note groove that uses tied 1/16th notes to create a syncopated bounce. The tied 1/16ths on the 2nd, 3rd, and 4th beats remove the down beat entirely, giving you a cool off beat groove to accent. The stretch between the 2nd and 6th frets is the trickiest part, so use your index and pinky, and momentarily reposition your thumb if needed to make the stretch smooth. Riffs like this are driven less by melody and more by the bounce and rhythm that lock in with the drums. Keep the feel in half time and move your body as you play to really lock into the groove.

Example 7i

Lastly, this riff combines drop-tuned power chord shapes with regular power chord shapes, and features hammer-ons and slides in the first three bars. The key element is the groove of the quintessential Bodom-style chugs between the fancier parts. The best picking pattern for these rhythms is down, up, up, as shown in the tab. Watch for the syncopation when you play a 1/16th note, then a 1/8th note, then another 1/16th note in sequence. The riff resolves with a trademark Laiho mid-riff arpeggio sequence. These are standard three-string shapes, but be mindful of the stretch from the 17th to the 12th fret on the sus2 arpeggio.

Example 7j

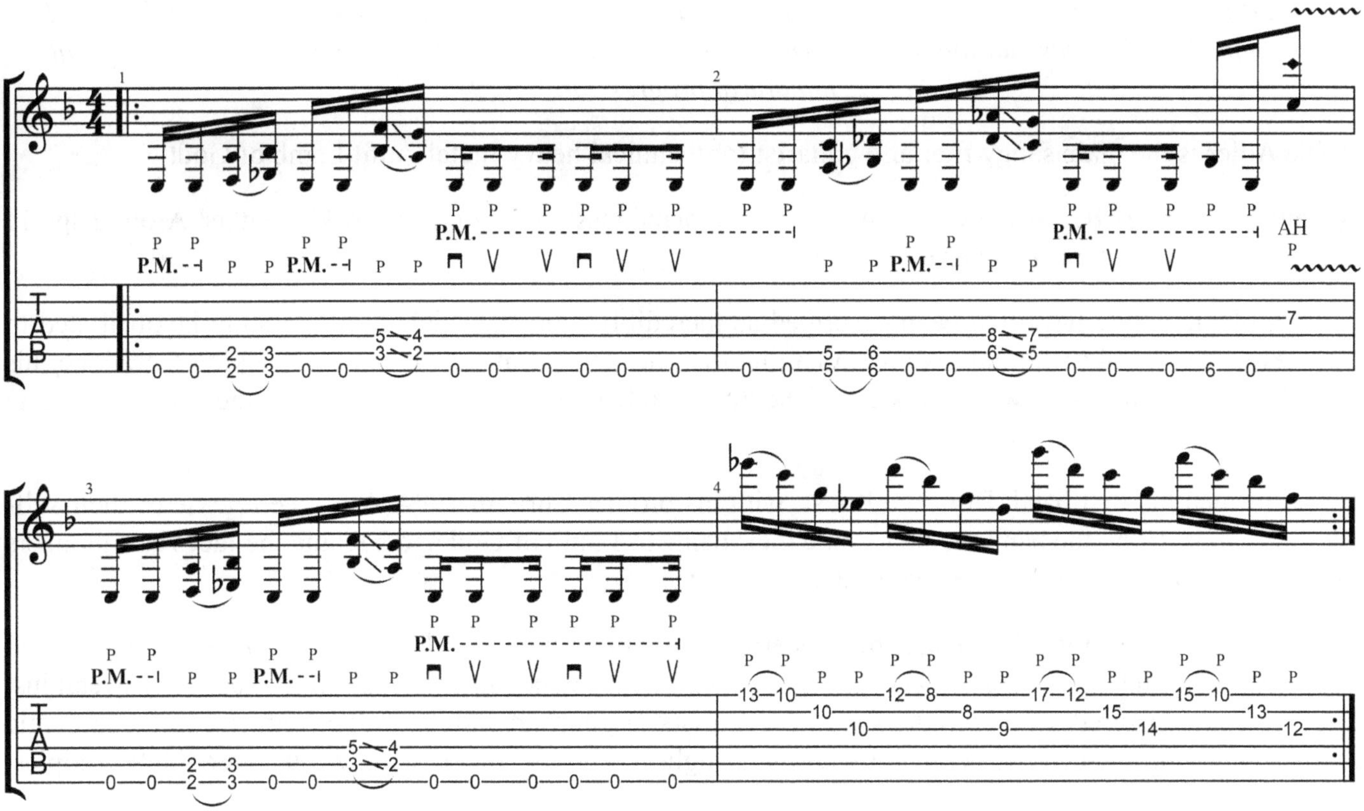

Chapter Eight – Willie Adler

"It all just grew out of comfortability and the way I wanted to speak through my guitar, and the way I accomplished that was manipulating my right hand into the way it's grown into. It was a very natural, unnatural progression."

Willie Adler is the main songwriter and guitarist for technical heavy metal outfit Lamb of God.

His musical journey began at a very young age, with piano lessons encouraged by his mother. Around age 11 he picked up the guitar and never looked back.

Adler's playing style has often been described as incredibly unique, which could possibly be attributed to him never having taken formal lessons. As a guitarist, he stands out for his unusual picking technique, his use of dissonant chords, as well as his use of the Phrygian Dominant scale in the riff-writing and songwriting process.

Willie formed his first band, Burn the Priest, with his brother Chris in 1994. After the release of their self-titled album in 1999, the band would change their name to Lamb of God and become the faces and pioneers of the New Wave of American Heavy Metal.

In 2004 Lamb of God would release the masterpiece album known as *Ashes of the Wake*, an album riddled with crazy riffs and interesting song arrangements, the likes of which late '90s and early 2000s Nu-Metal just didn't offer. It inspired a generation of young guitarists to jump up and down the fretboard in an acrobatic manner, while simultaneously becoming the band's highest selling album to date, selling over 400,000 copies.

For most his career, Willie has gravitated towards ESP guitars with Les Paul-type bodies, most notably the signature Willie Adler Eclipse, as well as the ESP Warbird. These guitars are often tricked out with Seymour Duncan pickups, and are paired with either Mark IV or Triple Crown Mesa Boogie Amp Heads.

Willie Adler's unique and unorthodox style has always been met with praise and criticism. He plays highly technical riffs and arrangements, yet his unusual picking style, stiff posture, and the way his forefinger wraps around his pick are all notable aspects of his playing.

Recommended Listening

As the Palaces Burn – Lamb of God (2003)

Ashes of the Wake – Lamb of God (2004)

Sacrament – Lamb of God (2006)

VII: Sturm und Drang – Lamb of God (2015)

Omens – Lamb of God (2022)

Willie Adler Riffs

This chapter's Willie Adler-themed material is built from ten riffs that form the sample tracks *Cremated Rednecks* and *Valley of Shadows*.

The first of five riffs in *Cremated Rednecks* is built on Lamb of God's signature guitar gallop double-kick feel, made up of two 1/16th notes followed by a 1/8th note.

To keep the riff interesting, the gallops are broken up with single notes, power chords, and major 6ths. The trickiest parts are the whole-step gaps of four frets between the 12th and 8th, 11th and 7th, and 10th and 6th frets. These stretches between index and pinky are big, so keep your fretting hand thumb in line with your middle finger for the most efficient reach.

Example 8a

Here's a lick that makes full use of Willie's plump, Hetfield-style downstrokes to build aggressive, heavy chord progressions. Play everything with downstrokes, paying attention to when chords are palm-muted and when they're not. The goal is to create strong dynamics between the chugs and the chords you want to stand out.

Example 8b

Next you'll play a riff that opens with a whole-step key change, giving the listener a break from the droning drop D note – a handy trick to remember for your own writing. It also leans heavily on an off beat 1/8th note early entry, shown in every bar by the tied notes. The riff has a very open sound thanks to a loose, unmuted picking hand.

Example 8c

This riff focuses on Lamb of God's trademark tense chugs spliced with D Phrygian Dominant. It is highly dynamic, so be precise about when you open and close your palm mutes. Make sure the gallop on the 3rd beat of bars one, three, and five is played with accuracy and aggression. The D Phrygian Dominant scale is a mode of G Harmonic Minor, and these scales often have big stretches, especially in three note per string shapes. Use your pinky where you can, and follow the suggested fingering shown in the notation.

Example 8d

The final example in this group of five riffs mixes power chord chugs, single-note fills, and some downright evil sounding major and minor 6th chords. As mentioned in Example 8d, some riffs are simple but need close attention to dynamics. Keep a tense, palm-muted feel on bars one, two, five, and six, then open up on bars three, four, seven, and eight. Strict down picking will build tension, while switching to alternate strumming will give a more flowing, "loosey goosey" feel. Follow the recommended strumming pattern closely.

Example 8e

This riff is the first of five that make up the second sample track *Valley of Shadows*. It leans heavily on triplets and gallops. The gallops are notated as a triplet 1/8th note, followed by two triplet 1/16th notes, then resolving on another triplet 1/8th note. Play the rest of the riff entirely with downstrokes (thank you, James Hetfield) to keep the aggression and energy high. Keeping the gallop rhythms tight is almost impossible without the right picking pattern, so follow the picking directions in the tab closely.

Example 8f

This idea relies heavily on flat-fingered power chords and down-stroked chugs. One bar is particularly demanding as it shifts from a chugged chord idea to single note riffage. The quick slides and legato are fiddly but become manageable after a few play-throughs. Loop this bar on its own until you can link it smoothly with the previous ones.

Example 8g

Here's a line based on Willie's love of single note riffage, outlining chords, and Phrygian Dominant. I have placed the inferred chord names above the riff when they occur. As a creative assignment, try writing a Willie Adler-style riff that uses riff-based chordal inference.

Example 8h

Now you'll play a riff built mostly from single notes and pull-offs. All the odd bars use palm mutes, while the even bars open up, creating a dynamic shift from a tense build to something fiddly, melodic, and a bit looser. Watch out for the tricky scale shapes, especially in bars four and eight.

Example 8i

The final Willie Adler example riff has more of a straight feel than the previous four in this song. Willie and Mark Morton often do this to create a juxtaposition or curveball in bridge sections of Lamb of God tracks. The most technical parts are in bars four and eight, which can be tricky if your fretting hand fingering is inefficient. Using all four fingers, especially the pinky, will help you navigate demanding riffs like this.

Example 8j

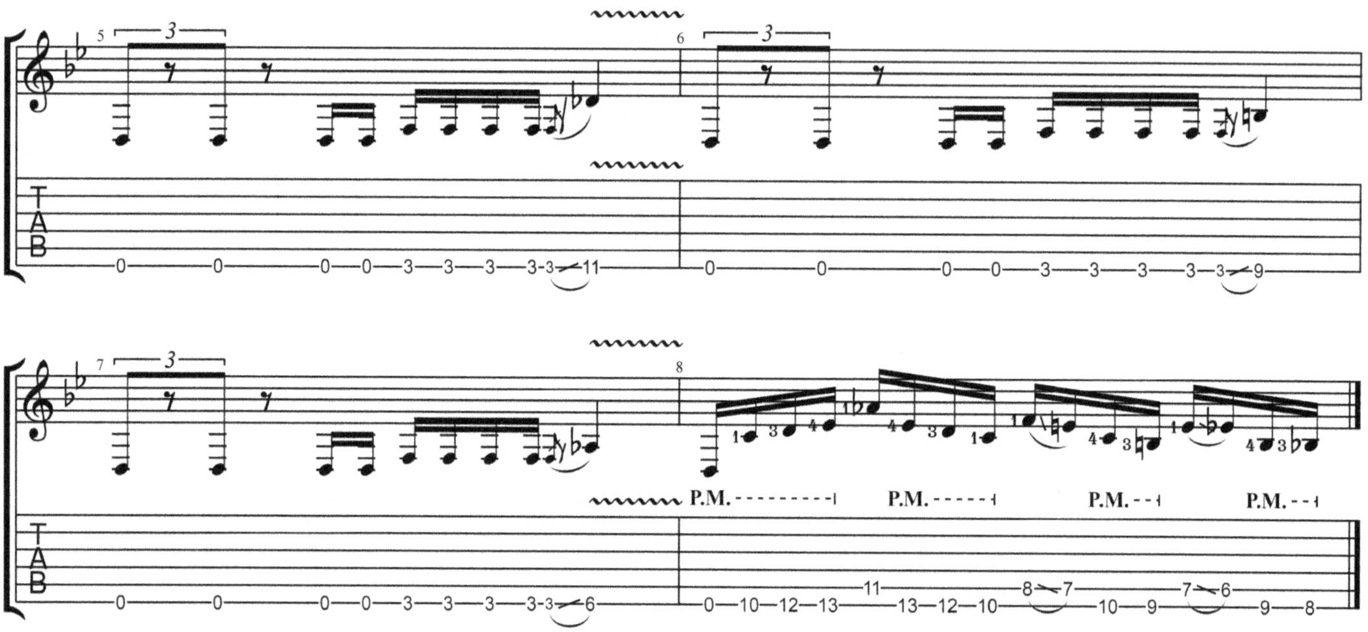
P.M.
P.M.
P.M.
P.M.

Chapter Nine – Adam Dutkiewicz

"The moment I started trusting my ear and not overthinking it, I actually started to write riffs I enjoy."

Adam Dutkiewicz was born on April 4, 1977, in Westhampton, Massachusetts, USA. He is known primarily for his guitar work and songwriting in the metalcore band Killswitch Engage, but has also worked as a producer with many other bands (including Shadows Fall, Parkway Drive, and All That Remains) throughout the 2000s and 2010s.

Adam's musical journey to becoming a guitarist was quite unusual. He studied bass guitar and production at Berklee College of Music, and he even played drums on Killswitch Engage's debut album. He attributes the guitarist he eventually became almost entirely to his idol, James Hetfield.

He started his first serious band, Aftershock, in 1999, which eventually evolved into Killswitch Engage. Killswitch Engage achieved great success with their 2004 album *The End of Heartache*, which sold around 600,000 copies. Their follow-up album *As Daylight Dies* sold 1.15 million copies worldwide, bringing their otherwise niche metalcore genre into the mainstream.

For most of his career in Killswitch Engage, Adam has predominantly used Caparison guitars, which in shape are not too dissimilar to ESP, Ormsby, or Jackson super-strat designs. These guitars are held in high regard in the metal/metalcore community for sounding tight and heavy, as well as being easy to play. Adam usually pairs them with EMG active pickups, typically the 81, 85, or 89 models.

Interestingly, Adam changes amp heads quite frequently, varying from Laney to Marshall to Peavey. This suggests that most of his signature sound comes from his guitar tone and pickups, and of course, from his own fingers.

Despite his hilarious onstage attire and over-the-top persona, Adam Dutkiewicz is an introspective, intelligent, and naturally talented musician.

Recommended Listening

Alive or Just Breathing – Killswitch Engage (2002)

The End of Heartache – Killswitch Engage (2004)

The Hymn of a Broken Man – Times of Grace (2011)

Disarm the Descent – Killswitch Engage (2013)

Atonement – Killswitch Engage (2019)

Adam Dutkiewicz Riffs

This chapter's Dutkiewicz-themed material is split into two groups of five riffs, forming the example tracks *Your Hex* and *Pain Ends Sorrow*. Both are played in Drop C tuning (C G C F A D).

The first five riffs are in 4/4, giving them a straight feel, while the second set highlights Adam's knack for moving seamlessly between 4/4 and 6/8.

In the first of five licks from *Your Hex*, you'll use 4- to 5-string chords with extra voicings to create sus2, major 7, minor 7, and add11 chords. Play them with a clean tone, adding reverb, delay, and subtle chorus for ambience. Rake each chord rather than strumming to keep the melancholy feel restrained. Make sure you're comfortable with flat-fingered, drop-tuned chord voicings.

Example 9a

Now you'll play a riff that arpeggiates the progression from Example 9a, focusing on the upper octave of each chord. Since it's played clean, let the notes bleed into one another as much as possible. This technique can work well in your own writing – to pair a big ringing chord with a second guitar adding small highlights over the top.

Example 9b

Here's a heavy version of the progression and melodic themes from Examples 9a and 9b, this time delivered with distortion, chunk, and attitude. Pay attention to the open strumming of five-string chords and how it contrasts with the palm-muted chugged notes. The riff resolves in bar eight with signature Adam D arpeggiated chords that bleed into each other, showing his love for suspended 2nds and the slight dissonance of add11 chords.

Example 9c

In Example 9d, you'll play a mix of open notes, hammer-ons, and inverted 5th double-stops. Keep the pace up, as the riff is mostly 1/16th notes, and aim for consistent speed when switching between picked and hammered notes. This riff is a great workout for your pinky and for building coordination between your pinky and index finger. Two three-fret gaps will help develop this stretch: one from the 13th to the 10th fret, and another from the 1st to the 4th fret.

Example 9d

In the final riff of the *Your Hex* sample track, you'll play an idea that shows Adam's love for riffs built around chordal movement. The progression outlines triads with a moving pedal root note in each chord. The toughest part is the four-fret stretches. Keep your fretting hand thumb on the back of the neck, roughly halfway between your index and pinky. Avoid a 45-degree wrist angle and use my patented *Taco grip method*. I.e., it's like holding a taco without spilling your beans and spicy meat all over the floor.

Example 9e

The next five riffs are also in Drop C tuning, but this set has a more melancholy (and at times eviller!) vibe than the last. Together, they form the sample track *Pain Ends Sorrow*. To start, you will play a chugged power chord motif that leans heavily on downstrokes for plumpness and aggressive palm muting. The trickiest part is the tied notes from bar three to bar four, forming an arpeggiated Bbsus2 and C dyad. These stretches call for careful thumb placement and solid pinky strength. I have put the fingering above the notation for that bar, and I insist you use it.

Example 9f

The following riff is built around Adam's love of hammer-ons and melodic, bleeding arpeggiated chords. The challenge here comes from the galloped open notes and the odd placement of some mid-bar note ties. I've indicated my suggested picking directions in the notation for bars one, three and five, where the most complex rhythms occur.

Finally, the last two bars use the Bbsus2 and Cadd11 arpeggios. They aren't particularly fast but the stretches are quite awkward. Make sure all the notes ring out and bleed into one another to keep it Killswitchy. Both chord shapes are led by the pinky finger and will require very accurate hand-arching technique.

Example 9g

In the next riff, you'll play an idea based on a classic Adam D time signature change to 6/8. There's a finger-twister in the first bar that reappears a few times in this mini-etude. Start with a barred index finger, then shift to your middle. Although this isn't the most technical riff in the book, be mindful of the dynamics created by the palm mutes and follow the dynamics marked in the notation.

Example 9h

In the next riff, you'll use extra heavy inverted 5th power chords to create a massive breakdown. In drop tuning, the fingering for an inverted 5th looks like a minor 3rd chord, essentially an upside-down power chord. Keep these chords tight, and avoid pressing too hard, as that can bend them out of tune and take away their heaviness.

Example 9i

Finally, here's a riff based on a quintessential Killswitch Engage clean bridge or outro section. Use a clean tone and consider adding subtle effects like chorus, reverb, and a relatively dry delay. Similar to Example 9h, this section shifts to a 6/8 time signature and is not very difficult, but it needs to be played with the right swing. In the sample track, this section is harmonised in 3rds. That is not particularly hard to do, but it is a simple way to turn an idea into something with more depth and emotion.

Example 9j

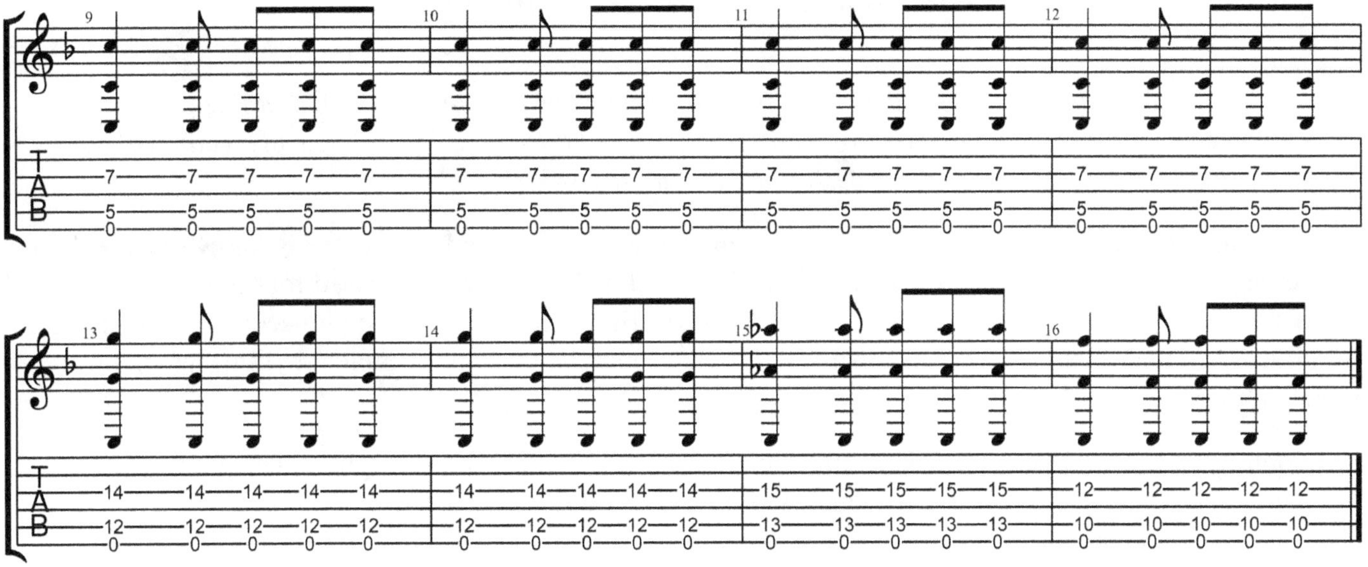
9
10
11
12
T
A
B
13
14
15
16
T
A
B

Chapter Ten – Misha Mansoor

"When you are a band in the music industry, you are always dancing between that line of art and commerce. You are trying to monetise your creativity as best and as efficiently as you can without destroying the artistic side."

Misha Mansoor was born on October 31, 1984, in Bethesda, Maryland, USA. He is known primarily for his guitar work and songwriting in the band Periphery, but he has also been praised for his work in Haunted Shores as well as his solo releases under the pseudonym Bulb. He is one of the pioneers of the djent genre, introducing technical riffs, odd time signatures, intricate compositions, and complex rhythms into mainstream metal culture.

At around the age of 13 or 14, Misha (like many of us) acquired the holy grail of beginner guitars: an instrument he describes as a crappy nylon string guitar. His story isn't one of a child prodigy with an early start or a natural knack for the instrument.

Misha formed his first band in 2004, a project with a friend simply called Bulb. He later turned Bulb into a solo project, even adopting Bulb as his own moniker. Bulb released self-produced demos on a music-based social community called SoundClick.

Periphery formed in 2005 and went through a bunch of line-up changes and extensive touring. This hectic period repeatedly delayed the release of their first full-length album, so their self-titled debut *Periphery* didn't come out until 2010, a full five years after the band's inception.

Periphery's first album was met with praise for its technical proficiency, heavy riffs, and innovations that helped cement the modern era of progressive metal. With Misha at the forefront, he went from being a relatively unknown bedroom musician to a metal household name in just a few years.

Even though the band is relatively obscure in a niche genre, Periphery achieved great success with the release of *Periphery IV: Hail Stan*. The album sold 9,600 copies in its first week and was even nominated for a Grammy.

Misha is currently signed to Jackson Guitars, and he primarily uses his signature Jackson Juggernaut HT6 and HT7 models. His huge tone can be attributed to Peavey and Marshall amplifier heads, as well as Fractal Audio's Axe-Fx II processor.

Misha's approach to his instrument and his elaborate compositions (both in and out of Periphery) displays intelligence and a unique perspective on how he approaches his career as a full-time musician.

Recommended Listening

Periphery – Periphery (2010)

Periphery II: This Time It's Personal – Periphery (2012)

Periphery III: Select Difficulty – Periphery (2016)

Periphery IV: Hail Stan – Periphery (2019)

Misha Mansoor Riffs

This chapter's Misha Mansoor-inspired material is split into two sets of five riffs, which form the sample tracks *Arrested Envelopment* and *Yu-Yevon*. The songs are in Drop C tuning (C G C F A D) and Drop G# tuning (G# D# G# C# F# A# D# on a 7-string), respectively.

In the first of five Drop C riffs from *Arrested Envelopment*, you'll combine three-string drop-tuned spread triads, string-crossing riffage, and arpeggiations. These riffs involve quick shifts up and down the neck, so use the open notes between fills and chords to give yourself just enough time for smooth transitions.

Example 10a

In this riff, you'll play a chorus or pre-chorus idea built from rising octaves and drop-tuned triads. A non-diatonic "curveball" chord appears in bar seven to introduce an outside sound, and bar eight ends with a whacky fill to resolve the riff. Most of it is 1/8th notes, which sound more aggressive when played entirely with downstrokes. Alternate picking can add an unwanted sway that reduces tension, so it's a good reminder to think about strumming direction in your own writing.

Example 10b

Now move on to Example 10c. This riff focuses on melodic arpeggiations with bleeding notes and uses only the first three strings. Keep your fretting hand fingers arched so the open first string can drone throughout.

Example 10c

Here's a riff that features a few odd meters and extended-range chords, riddled with melodic information and density. There are a few fills that occur over some 5/8 bars (a classic prog/tech-metal trick to make the rhythm unpredictable and throw the listener's ear off). I want you to concentrate mostly on the five-string chords and use the fingering in the notation.

Example 10d

Next you'll play a riff inspired by Misha's love of dissonance and chaos, created with outside semitone clashes and augmented or diminished chord-based note choices. Most of it is in 1/16th notes to cram in as much melodic detail as possible and overwhelm the listener. There's also a surprise 7/8 section in bar three, so watch out for that!

Example 10e

The next five riffs are in Drop G# and require a 7-string guitar. Together, they form the sample track *Yu-Yevon*. Start with open notes on the low 7th string, jumping octaves and playing octave chords with 1/4 note bends. Watch for the quick time signature change to 3/4 in bars four and eight.

Example 10f

In Example 10g, the riff takes a similarly chaotic approach to Example 10e. The fast 1/16th hammer-ons may look flashy, but the real challenge is in its djenty feel and the precise picking directions that shape the groove. Follow the marked picking directions in the notation closely.

Example 10g

In this example, we'll look at a riff that combines multiple odd meters, dead notes, and a strong focus on the djenting technique. This section tests your counting skills as much as your guitar playing. Before picking up your guitar, try tapping the meters on a table at 120bpm, counting in 1/8th notes. The meter order is 7/8, 7/8, 6/8, then 4/4, repeating through bars five to eight. Your counting should look like this:

1 2 3 4 5 6 7

1 2 3 4 5 6 7

1 2 3 4 5 6

1 2 3 4 5 6 7 8

Good luck and happy tech djenting.

Example 10h

This riff is based on Misha's use of spread dyads, which pair a root note with its 10th, the major or minor 3rd an octave higher. On a 7-string guitar, these intervals require solid thumb placement to manage the stretches. In situations like this, I use the Taco grip, with my fretting hand thumb positioned halfway between my index and pinky.

Example 10i

Lastly, here's a lick using arpeggio-based riffs inspired by the approach used in Periphery's *Marigold*. This method is a great way to make a melodic riff sound low and chuggy without becoming boring or feeling like a straight arpeggiated triad. The riff shifts quickly from single notes to chords, and these transitions work best when you use open notes and dead notes to bridge from one idea to the next.

Example 10j

Conclusion

Congratulations, you made it to the end! If your fingers are still attached and your amp isn't literally smoking, that's a win. Take a moment to appreciate what you've just accomplished: a whirlwind tour through decades of rock and metal riff history, from the birth of heavy metal in the '70s to the cutting-edge complexity of today.

You didn't just learn 100 riffs, you've picked up the habits, tricks, and flair of ten legendary guitarists along the way. Whether you're now bending notes with extra Sabbath-y gloom, galloping through thrash rhythms with a Hetfield sneer, or tossing in a quirky odd-time break that would make Misha Mansoor crack a smile, you've expanded your musical toolkit and then some. Give yourself a horns-up – you've earned it.

Throughout these chapters, you didn't just copy riffs note for note, either – you gained an insight into why they work and how these players think. You've basically been jamming with a hall of fame of guitar mentors, and now their influence flows in your playing. This book was never meant to be about turning you into a clone – it's giving you the tools to develop your own voice, using their wisdom as a springboard. Maybe a little of Tony's doom, Jeff and Dave's chromatic chaos, or Misha's disregard for keeping meters now shows up in your riffs. If it does, good. Embrace it, mix it up, and create something new.

Where do you go from here? The journey never really ends. That's the beautiful and mildly maddening truth about the guitar. You've got 100 new riffs under your fingers. Use them as starting points. Try writing your own riffs or full songs inspired by what you've learned. What happens if you take a Mustaine rhythm and play it with an EVH swing? Or add Laiho-style harmonies to a Hetfield chug? Experiment. Some ideas will be glorious; others will flop hilariously. Regardless, the process and the endeavour is worth doing.

Also, dive into the recommended listening for each chapter. Go learn *War Pigs*, *Holy Wars*, or *South of Heaven* and notice how the riffs you've practiced pop up in context. That kind of connection sticks with you. Most importantly, keep it fun. Even the most brutal, complex metal has room for humour and joy.

Rock and metal guitar are rebellious, exuberant, and deeply personal. When you hit a wall (because we all do), just remind yourself why you started. Maybe it was to light up a stage. Maybe it was because a loud amp on a bad day makes everything better. Whatever your reason, hold onto it. Throw on a favourite record, feel the love for this ridiculous and wonderful instrument, and jump back in.

Thank you for letting me be your guide on this riff-heavy, laugh-filled journey. It's been a blast for me and, probably less so for your neighbours who had to endure your Slayer phase. Now go. Shred. Crank your amp. Embrace the glorious noise.

Keep it large and keep it loud.

Big love!

Chris

\m/